LIFE'S LITTLE INSTRUCTION BOOK™
— for —
INCURABLE
Romantics

H. JACKSON BROWN, JR.
AND
ROBYN F. SPIZMAN

Rutledge Hill Press · Nashville, Tennessee
A THOMAS NELSON COMPANY

Published by Rutledge Hill Press, a Thomas Nelson Company, P.O. Box 141000, Nashville, Tennessee 37214.

Text and cover design by Bruce Gore

Library of Congress Cataloging-in-Publication Data is available.

ISBN 1-55853-833-X

Printed in the United States of America
1 2 3 4 5 6 7 8 9—05 04 03 02 01 00

www.instructionbook.com

ACKNOWLEDGMENTS

OUR GRATEFUL THANKS to all who contributed to this collection of romantic hints and advice and especially to those who touched and inspired us with their own personal love stories: Kimberly Adams, Carla Archuletta, Heather Aveson, Janet Berg, Mildred Bixler, Joyce Blaylock, Kathy Carmichael, Nancy Cohen, Wendy Dickinson, Julie Doherty, Iris Feinberg, Lynda Flury, Doug Freedman, Genie Freedman, Jack Freedman, Phyllis Freedman, Tracy Freeman, Norma Gordon, Jeannie Halford, Heather Hall, Lynne Halpern, Christa Huggins, Jay Janco, Bethany Kirby, Elizabeth Laine, Carla Lovell, Ruth McAlister, Doris Marks, Cara Mattison, Katie Morgan, Dolly Norman, Edward Norman, Louise Prochuska, Marie Reedy, Diane Riley, Jane Ritz, Elizabeth Rousakis, Ashley Sparks, Sam Spizman, Ann Marie Stevens, Amelia Stipek, Bettye Storne, Paige Trager, Jianne Verrill, Ava Wilensky, and Lindsay Whiteway.

IMAGINE A WORLD without love and romance. No love poems or love letters. No Romeo and Juliet. No Clark Kent and Lois Lane. No Mickey and Minnie. No heart-shaped boxes of chocolates or long-stemmed roses that say, "I'll love you forever." No heights of passion or depths of despair.

In love, we are at our best and our silliest. In love, we are the only two people on the planet, certain that no others have felt the same way we do. Love has many faces. Young love is wild and outrageous, laughing at moderation and blinding us to common sense. Mature love is composed and sustaining; a celebration of companionship, and trust. It is the lucky man and woman who experience both.

The poet John Dryden called love "a noble madness." To Cole

Porter, it was "that old black magic." The Beatles convinced us that "all you need is love."

But love withers if left alone. Like a garden it needs tending every day. Adorning a loving relationship regularly with creative and thoughtful romantic gestures takes time, practice, and commitment. And yet, in another way, romance is surprisingly simple. As one of our contributors expressed it, "Being incurably romantic is simply the ability of one person to make another feel cherished."

It is our hope that this book will inspire you to find new ways to make the love of your life feel more treasured and adored.

We urge you to begin today. Your making the first move is the key. The result will be a relationship refreshed with new possibilities and promise.

Instructions
for People
Really in Love

1. Say, "I love you" first and say it often.

2. Record the date you first met and celebrate it every year.

3. Always give a loving welcome home.

4. Kiss each other passionately in a crowded elevator.

5. Occasionally, hide a little present under your loved one's pillow.

6. Have a photo taken of the two of you together on each anniversary.

7. Tell your sweetheart that the sound of his or her voice is the most endearing sound in all the world.

8. Listen with your ears and eyes, but most importantly listen with your heart.

9. Be specific when you give a compliment.

10. Clean out and vacuum your mate's car.

11. Hold hands at your high school reunion. Everyone will notice.

The sound of a kiss is not so loud as that of a cannon, but its echo lasts a great deal longer.

– Oliver Wendell Holmes

12. Choose a romantic song that's "your song."

13. Look at your wedding photos together every anniversary.

14. Be each other's cheerleader.

15. If you are the first to read the newspaper, leave it neatly folded and in order.

16. Be your mate's best friend.

17. Create a special signal that only the two of you understand that says, "I love you."

18. Compliment each other in front of your friends.

19. Compliment each other in front of your kids.

20. Cut out the comics that make you laugh and share them.

21. On Valentine's Day, surprise your mate with a treasure hunt. You be the treasure.

22. Always try to reserve the same table at your favorite restaurant.

23. Bring each other breakfast in bed.

24. Give her a cuddly teddy bear when a hug is needed and you can't be there.

25. Ask each other out on dates.

26. When traveling together, hold hands every time your plane takes off and lands.

For you see, each day I love you more. Today more than yesterday and less than tomorrow.

– *Rosemonde Gerard*

27. Don't forget the little courtesies like putting the cap back on the toothpaste.

28. Learn to give the world's best back rub and foot massage.

29. After your sweetheart's had a hard day, prepare a relaxing bubble bath for her illuminated by the warm glow of vanilla scented candles.

30. Remember the special treats your partner loves and always have back-ups in your pantry.

31. Check in on each other every day by phone. Always end the conversation by whispering, "I love you."

32. Take a walk together in a light spring rain.

33. Remember, it's sometimes best to just listen and to resist giving advice.

34. The next time you're at a flea market, buy your mate a toy or game he or she loved as a child.

35. Create a video of why you and everyone else loves your mate and surprise her with it on her birthday.

36. Have a picture of the two of you hugging or kissing. Place it where you can see it every day.

37. Ask your spouse what he or she treasures most about you.

38. Put a scrumptious surprise in the refrigerator with your loved one's name on it.

To love someone is to see a miracle invisible to others.

– *Francois Mauriac*

39. Ask your mate what three things you could do that would make him happier.

40. When your partner speaks or performs in front of an audience, be there front row center.

41. Steer clear of restaurants with strolling musicians.

42. Make a big deal out of what your sweetheart does right.

43. Reminisce about the first time you kissed each other. If possible, return to the very same spot.

44. Be passionate about being passionate.

45. Go to the movies your mate wants to see.

46. Tape your mate's favorite television programs when she or he is working late.

47. Frame a favorite greeting card from your loved one and put it in a prominent place.

48. When you're unsure of what to do or say, give a hug.

49. This weekend pretend you're staying at a swanky hotel and secretly place a piece of fancy foil-wrapped chocolate on your sweetheart's pillow.

50. Write "I love you" and your sweetheart's name on a sandy beach.

51. Keep an extra key to your partner's car hidden in your wallet in case he loses his.

52. Take time to learn more about your mate's favorite teams.

53. Use self-sticking notes to form a big heart on your bathroom mirror. Write ILY on all the notes before sticking them in place.

54. Have a romantic dinner catered just for the two of you at home.

*I*t is best to love wisely, no doubt; but to love foolishly is better than not to be able to love at all.

— *William Makepeace Thackeray*

55. Find romantic spots to visit—a shaded park bench, a secluded garden, any place you both love—and go there often.

56. Rent a portable billboard and announce your love with an endearing message.

57. Prove daily to your sweetheart that your relationship is a top priority.

58. Purchase a selection of romantic greeting cards and give one to your spouse every hour on the day of your anniversary.

59. Sneak your mate's car out and bring it back washed and filled with gas.

60. Make sure everything except you is turned off before going to bed.

61. Never criticize or correct your mate in public.

62. Keep each other's secrets a secret.

63. Compliment your mate's sense of humor.

64. Write down your mate's telephone messages as accurately as you do your own.

65. When your sweetheart wants to dance, dance.

66. Install a carbon monoxide and radon detector.
    This might not sound romantic but it's
    definitely an act of love.

67. Leave a romantic message on your mate's
    answering machine.

There is no surprise more magical than the surprise of being loved; it is God's finger on man's shoulder.

— *Charles Morgan*

68. Always call to make sure your loved one gets home safely.

69. Tape a love note to a five-dollar bill and slip it into your loved one's wallet.

70. Look at each other's high school annuals and try not to laugh.

71. Ask your partner to make a wish list. Use it for gift ideas for those special occasions.

72. Serve him heart-shaped French toast in bed.

73. Surprise your mate by doing the one chore she hates the most.

74. Make a wish on the evening star together.

75. Whisper "I love you" in your mate's ear during a romantic moment in a movie.

76. If your loved one is afraid or overly concerned about something, find professionals who can help.

77. Take a horse and carriage ride through Central Park during a winter snow.

78. Remember the ABCs of love: Always Be
    Considerate.

79. Call each other in the middle of the day just to
    say, "Hello, I love you. I can't wait to see you."

80. Buy your sweetheart three books by his favorite
    author.

A woman unsatisfied must have luxuries. But a woman who loves a man would sleep on a board.

– *D.H. Lawrence*

81. Give your mate a Valentine card on the 14th of *every* month.

82. Write him a love note in his appointment book.

83. Regardless of what you are doing, show attention to your sweetheart whenever she enters the room.

84. Remember that the heights of romance are determined by the depths of trust.

85. Bite your tongue the next time you feel compelled to say something to your mate that's not positive and loving.

86. Never argue in the bedroom. Have your quarrels in another room of the house.

*Love comforteth
like sunshine after rain.*

– *William Shakespeare*

87. Don't be ashamed to let your loved one see you cry.

88. Be frank with your mate about what turns you on and what turns you off.

89. Prepare a snack pack when your love is taking a long road trip. Fill it with his favorite goodies and a homemade "I Love You" note.

90. Know your sweetheart's favorite song, color, fragrance, movie, book, snack, flower, dessert, and romantic destination.

91. Learn to say, "I love you" in French, Spanish and Italian.

92. Place a single-stem flower on your mate's pillow with a loving note.

93. The next time you visit a restaurant that has booths, sit side-by-side.

94. When she steps from her bath or shower, offer her a towel you've warmed in the clothes dryer.

95. Spell out "I ♥ you" in clean socks on the bed to welcome your sweetheart home.

96. When your partner is traveling out of town, call the hotel's concierge and have a special treat delivered to her room as a surprise.

97. Give each other something made of cashmere.

98. When you need affection, don't make your partner guess. Ask!

99. Celebrate your better half's half birthday with half a cake, half a card, and all of you!

100. Give your sweetheart a love list of the ten things you most admire about him or her.

101. Never say, "I told you so," even if you did.

102. Don't compare your relationship to anyone else's.

There is nothing holier, in this life of ours, than the first consciousness of love — the first fluttering of its silken wings.

— *Henry Wadsworth Longfellow*

103. Flirt, but only with each other.

104. Go to an afternoon movie together.

105. Accompany your mate to important doctor's appointments. Take notes and ask questions to make sure you both understand the situation, treatment, and prognosis.

106. Never greet or leave each other without a kiss.

107. Brag about each other every chance you get.

108. Make a contribution to The American Heart Association on Valentine's Day in honor of your partner. Tell him you were inspired by his heart of gold.

109. Purchase a pair of special dinner plates just for the two of you. Save them for special romantic occasions.

110. When building a new home or adding on, write both of your initials and the date in wet concrete.

111. Go to a lot of trouble on special occasions even if your loved one says not to.

112. Ask your honey what you've done together during the past month that he or she has enjoyed the most. Do it again.

113. Send your sweetheart flowers for no reason at all.

114. Make a big I LOVE YOU sign and place it inside the windshield of her car.

115. On a bright starry night, lie on a blanket in a grassy field and talk about your hopes and dreams.

116. Show respect for your mate's opinion even when you disagree.

117. When you're apart, read romantic poetry to each other over the phone.

If you have it, you don't need to have anything else, and if you don't have it, it doesn't much matter what else you have.

– *James M. Barrie*

118. Sponsor a garden in your sweetheart's honor at a senior citizen retirement home.

119. Kiss your partner before leaving for work, even if she's still asleep.

120. Visit a do-it-yourself ceramic store and paint "I Love You" coffee mugs for each other.

121. Compliment something about every meal your sweetheart prepares.

122. Recreate your first date as to the time, place, and what you wore.

123. Have a beautiful flower arrangement awaiting when your loved one returns from a trip.

124. Kidnap your mate in the middle of the day for a picnic in the park.

125. Remember the magic of the words "please," "thank you," and "I'm sorry."

126. At social functions, remind your sweetheart that she's the most gorgeous woman in the room.

127. Reread your old love letters to each other.

128. Make sure your honey always has an up-to-date map when traveling to a new destination. Visit www.mapquest.com to print out instant directions.

129. Tell your children why you love their mom so much.

*L*ove is like the measles; all the worse when it comes late.

– *Douglas Jerrold*

130. Take tango lessons together.

131. Be the first to reach for your loved one's hand when you're walking side-by-side.

132. Remember the song that was played as you first danced as husband and wife at your wedding reception. Request it whenever you go dancing.

133. Tell your spouse he or she is absolutely the best in the world at something. Be specific.

134. Put a romantic CD in your partner's car that will begin playing as soon as the engine starts.

135. Plan a romantic get-away together and take care of all the details.

136. Remember that love is like a beautiful garden. It needs constant care and attention.

137. Talk about the feelings you had when you first saw each other.

138. Tie balloons to your mailbox on your love's birthday.

139. Let your smile be the first thing your loved one sees after a long day.

140. Give your mate a neat nickname.

141. Share important news first with your mate.

142. Be the first to suggest doing something you know your sweetheart loves.

143. Even when you're angry, always treat each other with respect.

144. Never give her an anniversary gift that has to be plugged in.

145. Remember that every day you have the power to brighten your sweetheart's life by word, if not by deed.

146. Give her a ceramic box filled with Hershey Kisses. Attach a card that reads, "Open in case of an emergency" (that is, when you're not around to give her a real kiss).

147. Present a flower bouquet one stem at a time: one on the pillow, one in the closet, one in the toothbrush holder, one in the briefcase, one in the car, all throughout the day.

*T*hose who love deeply never grow old; they may die of old age, but they die young.

– *Sir Arthur Wing Pinero*

148. Never suggest he might be losing his hair.

149. Never suggest she needs to lose weight.

150. When your partner is overworked and overwhelmed, ask what you can do to help.

151. Set out his daily morning medicine.

152. Kiss your sweetheart at ten o'clock. When he asks why, say it's because he's a perfect ten.

153. Out of the blue, tell your partner he is the most interesting person you know.

154. Discover something that always makes your loved one laugh.

155. Have your mate's tires and car checked on a regular basis.

156. Display your wedding portrait in a place of honor.

157. When your sweetheart is having lunch with friends, surprise her with a greeting card saying how much you love her. Have the waiter deliver it.

158. Remind your spouse to use seat belts. Tell her to pretend that it's a hug from you.

159. Pamper your sweetie with hot tea and honey when she has a cold or sore throat.

160. Plan an I LOVE YOU day for no special reason and make it a yearly holiday.

That is the true season of love, when we believe that we alone can love, that no one could ever have loved so before us, and that no one will love in the same way after us.

— *Goethe*

161. Create spaces in your togetherness.

162. Overdo something your mate loves: tons of chocolate, hundreds of licorice jellybeans, boxes of Milano cookies.

163. Always open the car door for her. Help her with her coat. Pull out the chair for her at restaurants.

164. Buy ice cream cones; sit in the park or mall and people watch.

165. Splurge on luxurious sheets and bed coverings.

166. Remember that true love is when the other person's happiness is more important that your own.

167. Laugh at your beloved's jokes even if you've heard them before.

168. Occasionally watch your sweetheart's favorite TV programs—even if you don't enjoy them.

169. Create a romantic way to celebrate the season's first snowfall.

170. When dining out, call ahead and ask the chef to come out and introduce himself to *your* favorite chef!

171. Share your dreams.

172. Share your fears.

173. Share your desserts.

A kiss is a lovely trick designed by nature to stop speech when words become superfluous.

– *Ingrid Bergman*

174. Let your sweetheart overhear you saying wonderful things about her.

175. Regardless of how upset you may be with each other, never sleep apart.

176. Take some silly photos of the two you in an instant photo booth.

177. Never discuss past loves.

178. Keep your promises.

179. Forgive quickly.

180. Kiss slowly.

181. Revisit the location where you said, "I do."

182. If you and your partner have a serious disagreement, say, "I'm sorry you're upset. What can I do to make you feel better?" These are healing, magical words.

183. When picking up your sweetheart at the airport, be waiting at the gate with a bouquet of balloons or flowers.

184. Next Valentine's Day buy an extra bag of the small heart-shaped conversation candies (those with the messages on them) for romantic use throughout the year.

185. Even if you don't cook, find a source for home-made chicken soup and serve it in a pretty bowl when your sweetheart is feeling under the weather.

What is love? I have met in the streets a very poor young man who was in love. His hat was old, his coat worn, the water passed through his shoes and the stars through his soul.

– Victor Hugo (1802-1885)

186. Slow dance every chance you get.

187. When your love misplaces something in the house (wallet, car keys, etc.), stop what you're doing and help her or him look for it.

188. Carry a list of your mate's clothing sizes in your wallet.

189. Send your mother-in-law flowers on your spouse's birthday.

190. Spare no expense on your honeymoon or when celebrating your anniversary.

191. Find an activity or sport that you and your sweetie can participate in together.

192. When disagreements arise, avoid using the words
never and *always*.

193. Remember the magic of the words, "You look
fabulous!"

194. Be her hero and respond to her screams when she
sees a spider or any other creepy-crawler thing.

195. Share a Key West sunset.

196. Tell her when she has lipstick on her teeth.

197. Tell him when he has spots on his trousers.

198. Attach a sign on your car that reads, "still married and mighty proud of it" on your anniversary.

It is possible that a man can be so changed by love as hardly to be recognized as the same person.

— *Terence*

199. Remember that the quality of your relationship reflects the kind of care you give it.

200. Wrap yourselves in luxury with his-and-hers terrycloth bathrobes like those offered guests at swanky hotels.

201. When apologizing, don't ruin it with an excuse.

202. Follow this financial advice for a happy marriage: If it doesn't cost more that $25... If it doesn't hurt anyone... If you won't remember it one year from now... always say yes!

203. Never forget the three powerful resources you always have available to you; love, prayer, and forgiveness.

204. Cuddle more.

205. Caress more.

206. Comfort more.

207. When attending a wedding, hold your spouse's hand and silently renew your wedding vows.

208. Offer a solution when you bring up a problem.

209. Write a loving message on a sticky note and hide it in a book your partner is reading.

210. When your sweetheart phones you at work, take the call immediately regardless of how busy you are.

211. Sit down and talk with each other without any outside distractions when you arrive home from work.

212. Memorize your mate's favorite love poem and recite it at special romantic moments.

213. In difficult times, remember why you fell in love in the first place.

214. Watch the movie *Casablanca* together.

215. Wear proudly anything that she gives you that she's handmade.

216. Work on your marriage harder than you do on anything else.

217. Wink at each other across a crowded room.

218. Respect your sweetheart's time. Don't make him or her wait.

219. Go overboard and give her a month's supply of her favorite candy. Put it in an old-fashioned tin lunch box.

220. Remember that if it matters to your partner, it should matter to you.

221. When your partner travels, leave a message at his hotel greeting him and telling him how much you miss him.

222. Whisper unexpectedly, "How could I have ever been so lucky to have found you?"

223. Pray together.

224. Love deeply and passionately. You might get hurt, but it's the only way to live life completely.

225. Kiss her palm, and fold your kiss into her closed hand.

226. Never stop the wooing.

227. Count your blessings and start with each other.

Heart-warming
Stories of Romantic
Moments

When my husband was completing his medical fellowship, we were young parents with very little money. One night he took me out to a nice dinner. On the way home, we stopped at a beautiful home, which, to my surprise, was actually a bed and breakfast. We went in and my husband boldly asked if we could tour the estate. In one of the bedrooms he had already placed a bottle of champagne, a bouquet of flowers, chocolates, and a big box from Victoria's Secret. It was an anniversary I'll always remember.

— Iris

*W*hen my wife arrived home from work on her twenty-fifth birthday, she found a single red rose on each of the twelve steps leading up to our apartment. When she opened our door I greeted her by handing her another dozen. I surprised her again when she saw that both of our suitcases were already packed. We spent her birthday weekend in her favorite city sightseeing and dining in her favorite restaurants.

– Clint

*E*very time my husband and I take off or land in an airplane, he kisses my hand.

— *Robyn*

*D*uring our twenty-one years of marriage, my husband, who has exquisite taste, would find unique pieces of antique jewelry to give me on special occasions. Sadly, I lost my antique wedding band during my second pregnancy. I was devastated, because it held such special meaning for both of us.

Last year, while on vacation, we stopped to browse in a jewelry store and I found the second ring of my dreams. My husband secretly bought it as a surprise for our twentieth wedding anniversary. It turned out that the ring had been made in my husband's hometown of Stuttgart, Germany. Surely we were meant to own that ring.

– Carla

*S*ince I love to snack on Cracker Jacks, imagine my surprise when I found a ring that I had long admired inside the box. My husband placed the ring inside and then resealed the box so carefully that it appeared to have never been opened. To make things even sweeter, he had our names engraved on the ring. Now I always double-check the toy surprise when eating my Cracker Jacks.

— *Louise*

When we were in college, my boyfriend sent me a love letter on adding machine tape. It eventually unrolled to almost ten feet, and I loved every inch of it.

– *Phyllis*

*M*y fiancé and I attend graduate schools many miles apart. I love just hearing his voice, but the phone bills were really piling up. When I installed a computer disc he sent me in the mail, it was his voice saying, "I love you angel." Now every time I need to hear his voice, I turn on my computer and play the disc over and over.

— *Paige*

This might not sound romantic, but it was truly an act of love on my part. My husband let me redecorate our home with one exception – his Lazy Boy chair. I wanted to replace it or at least recover it, but I finally gave in and let him keep it the way it was. The new family room won't make *Architectural Digest,* but I can assure you that a contented husband sitting in his old beat-up chair is definitely preferable to a grouchy one frowning in a chair that is stylish.

– Elizabeth

*M*y husband loves the little notes I put in his lunch box telling him how much I love him. I also write romantic messages on the steamed-up mirror in the bathroom for him to see when he gets out of the shower.

— Jeannie

I had a boyfriend who was an English major at the U.S. Naval Academy. At first, he wrote poems for me. I called him my Knight in Shining Armor and he called me his Princess. We played it up in our letters, creating a wonderfully romantic fantasy. Our letters inspired him to write a stage play based on our romance. It is currently being considered as an off-Broadway production in New York.

— *Lindsay*

I've lived a very sheltered life and have always been a housewife. After my son went to college, I decided to enroll in night classes. My husband supported me wholeheartedly and I've always loved him for helping me to realize that it's never too late to challenge yourself with new ideas and possibilities.

– Mildred

$\mathcal{I}$ was on a flight to Los Angeles when the stewardess announced over the intercom that the person in seat number 21-B had won a prize. The prize was a rather ordinary looking little box but when the young woman passenger opened it she discovered a sparkling engagement ring and a note that read, "Will you marry me?" Her soon-to-be fiancé was waiting at the gate for her answer when we landed.

— *Norma*

My brother phoned his girlfriend and told her to be ready at five o'clock. A limousine picked her up and took her to a heliport in New York. He was waiting in the helicopter and as they flew over the Statue of Liberty at sunset, he asked her to marry him. When they landed they celebrated with a fabulous dinner at the famous Rainbow Room, sixty-five floors above Rockefeller Center.

– Ava

T once sent two dozen roses to my wife—one dozen on Valentine's Day and the second dozen the day after Valentine's Day. She didn't expect the second dozen.

– *Doug*

*M*y boyfriend and I love Luciano Pavarotti's rendition of *Nessun Dorma*. We listened to it for years without knowing the Italian words, but we just knew they had to be romantic and beautiful. Christmas was approaching, and I thought that a framed copy of the sheet music and English lyrics would make a wonderful present for him. I looked everywhere for a translator. The Italians who run the neighborhood pizza parlor even tried to help by calling relatives in Italy. Bits and pieces came out, but not enough. Ready to give up, I called an Italian girlfriend who was finally able to secure the English translation for me. The lyrics were indeed incredibly romantic. I framed it as planned and gave my boyfriend what he now calls his favorite gift ever.

– Ann Marie

My fiancé and I had been separated for more than three and a half years while he served in the army in the South Pacific during World War II. When he wrote to tell me he would be discharged at Fort Dix, New Jersey, on a certain date, I flew to New York City and surprised him at the airport where he was making connections to fly home. What a happy and romantic meeting that was!

– Jane

To celebrate my husband's thirty-fifth birthday, I made dinner reservations at one of our city's best restaurants and booked a lovely room in a downtown hotel. I also arranged for our babysitter to stay overnight. At the end of the meal the waiter handed me the bill and my husband the key to the hotel room. "Happy birthday, sir," he said with a smile. My husband couldn't believe I was able to keep so many secrets.

– Nancy

We had been married only a short time and were living in an apartment. At the season's first snowfall, all the cars were covered with snow and my husband wrote, "I Love You" on the back of ours. Everyone in the entire complex saw it.

— *Robyn*

$\mathscr{I}$ made a book for my boyfriend entitled, *I Love You Because...*. On each page I wrote a reason why I loved him and included an illustration. It was about 300 pages long. Every now and then I catch him reading it.

— Jennifer

*L*ast New Year's Eve, I was in the hospital for chemotherapy. The nurses, knowing how depressed I felt, allowed my boyfriend to spend the night in a reclining chair in my room. Earlier in the day he had called me to "confirm our reservations for Hotel Beaumont" (our nickname for the hospital). He arrived with a bottle of sparkling juice, noisemakers and party hats. He said a caterer (which turned out to be my mom) would soon arrive with other goodies. We played games and watched the ball drop at midnight. Then we toasted to a wonderful healthy and happy new year. His thoughtfulness made it my best New Year's Eve and it was so romantic.

My boyfriend never thought twice about sacrificing to make me happy and comfortable during my illness. When I cried, he made me laugh. When I grew tired and frustrated because of the treatments, he encouraged me. I'm much better now and our love for each other gets stronger every day.

– Heather

For many years my husband was a coal miner in Idaho. His shift began at 6 AM and so we had to get up at 4:30. He hated the Idaho winters, and on severely cold mornings, even when the thermometer reading would be way below zero, I would go out and start his old pickup truck and scrape the ice and snow off the windows. I wanted him to be warm and safe on his way to the mines.

We had grown up together in rural Illinois. He said that he knew I was the one for him when he was eleven years old. He told me this many times when we were kids, but I never believed him.

My dad died when I was thirteen and my mother sent me away to be a nanny in Chicago. My friend and I exchanged a letter every now and then, but I had no expectations of marriage. On my eighteenth birthday, I heard a knock on the door of the family I worked for. It was my future husband coming for me like he always said he would. We got married the next day.

– Elizabeth

*M*y husband often cuts fresh flowers from the garden when I'm not at home and places them in pretty vases in our bedroom or on my desk. It is a very sweet way for him to surprise me and tell me he loves me without words.

– *Carla*

My husband borrowed my Palm Pilot and programmed inside jokes and "I Love You" messages for different days. He also writes me beautiful letters that would make you cry. He even buys Viactiv Calcium Chews to insure that I'll get plenty of calcium. He sets one out for me every morning.

— *Cara*

$\mathcal{A}$ handsome young man spent several hours in my jewelry store looking at engagement rings before finally making his decision.

Later that evening, he took his girlfriend to dinner at Tavern on the Green in New York's Central Park. While they were eating, police stormed into the restaurant blowing whistles and yelling the guy's name. They surrounded his table and accused him of stealing merchandise. As he emptied his pockets, he pulled out a jewelry box. He opened it and handed it to his girlfriend. Then he got down on one knee and proposed. He had staged the entire scene. As you can guess, the other diners applauded when his girlfriend said, "Yes!"

– Lynne

*W*e were living in Baltimore when my husband and two of his friends planned a Valentine's Day dinner for their wives. The men did all the cooking and hired a violinist from the Baltimore Symphony Orchestra to serenade us with Mozart and Brahms while we ate. The dinners were unforgettable because between courses our husbands entertained us by reading love poems they had written. This has become an annual Valentine Day's tradition.

– Heather

For my thirtieth birthday, my boyfriend gave me a box that had a picture of a frying pan on the top of it. I almost had a fit thinking that a frying pan was absolutely the last thing that I wanted him to give me. "Go ahead, open the box," he said. I did, and instead of the dreaded frying pan, there was a little blue box from Tiffany's. And inside that was a gorgeous platinum ring. I was speechless.

– Kimberly

At twenty-eight, I was a young widow with a two-year-old daughter. My husband, a pilot in the Air Force, had died in a plane crash. After a while my sister introduced me to another pilot. We dated for more than a year before we married. During the ceremony he not only gave a ring to me but also presented a gold band to my little girl, her very own "wedding band."

Our daughter is now twenty-three years old and

she still wears that ring on a chain around her neck, along with a gold ring given to her at birth by her father. It means so much to see her wearing that necklace, a symbol of love, with rings from two men who are so very important to us both.

– Kathy

*O*nce when my husband was ill and in the hospital, he reached out to take my hand. I jumped up to tend to him. "I just wanted to touch you," he said.

– Dawn

*M*y husband sold his car to buy me an engagement ring. If that's not romantic, I don't know what is!

— *Marie*

The gift for a third wedding anniversary is supposed to be made of leather. My husband and I had just bought a farm, and so I gave him a pig. It didn't matter that the only leather was on the hoof because she was the cutest thing we had ever seen. We named her Greta Garbo because she had such great legs.

– Dolly

*L*ast year my husband filled my side of the bed with confetti that said "I Love You." I loved that!

— *Barbara*

*O*ne year while planning for Christmas and my husband's birthday, I wrote down all the little things he had said he wanted but which I knew he would never buy for himself. I gave one of these to him each month throughout the year as a "just because" gift. It wasn't an expensive thing to do but he realized that I loved him enough to listen attentively to everything he said.

— *Christa*

When my husband came home from a business trip, I met him at the door wearing a sarong and holding a pitcher of martinis. We were young then.

— *Diana*

The first time I went to visit my fiancé at her parent's home, she planned a whole week of fun things for us to do. She made cardboard tickets and coupons describing each activity including romantic dinners and back rubs. She put them in an envelope on my bed and each each morning I would choose three of the coupons. That's how we would spend the day.

– *Jay*

*A*s I think of all the interesting places we've been like Hawaii, Mexico, Yosemite National Park, San Francisco, Lake Tahoe, and the mountains of Colorado, one location stands out in my mind as the most romantic—our own home after the birth of our first daughter. It wasn't a time of physical passion or exotic travel, but my husband treated me like a queen. He brought the baby to me to nurse in bed, kept the house clean, and prepared my meals. He carefully and artistically arranged the food on the plate and the tray always had a little flower on it.

All this attention didn't last forever. I recovered from the Cesarean birth and began doing laundry, dishes, housework, and everything else we moms and wives do. But that feeling of being loved and pampered has always stayed with me. You know, love is really something you do, not something you say. My husband reminded me of that.

– Diane

Loving Advice
for a Long and Happy
Marriage

Always be polite to each other and remember the importance of saying "Please" and "Thank you." Treat him better than you treat your friends. Tell him you love him every day. Don't wait to celebrate your life together. Do it every day.

– *Amelia*

*A*gree to disagree sometimes. And listen when the other person talks. Really listen!

— *Ann*

*D*iscuss problems immediately. Don't think they will go away if you don't talk about them.

— *Donna*

Discuss the important things before you get married: how to discipline the children, how in-laws and money will be handled. And then always present a united front to your children in the decisions you make.

– Doris

*A*fter God, always put your husband first in your life regardless of how hard it might be sometimes. And when you have a quarrel, think about when you first met and started dating and how much in love you were. Before you know it, you will be making up.

— *Linda*

Know when to give the other person space. But when you're having an argument, stay in the room together until it is resolved.

– *Bethany*

*T*alk about everything together—your day, your life, your dreams, your future, your problems. Share the work and help each other. My husband and I spend time together and tell each other we love each other every day.

– Louise

*L*ook at the inner beauty. Establish trust from the start. Don't expect from your spouse what you are not willing to give in return.

– Sharon

*B*e happy and content with yourself first so that you can give these qualities to your mate. Always remember your first kiss and live to re-create it.

— *Laurie*

Compromise. Some things just aren't worth arguing about. I've been married 22 years and I know neither one of us is perfect. You need to choose battles carefully.

– Julie

*H*ave respect for each other's viewpoint. Husbands, send your wives flowers. Wives, make his favorite dishes. Say, "I love you," enthusiastically and often.

— Diana

The key word is tolerance. After you marry, you still have your own individuality and you will sometimes express it to the dismay of your mate. But if you practice tolerance and accept these differences as momentary glitches, your marriage will survive quite well.

— *Warren*

*N*ever tell him he's like his mother when he's being obnoxious.

— *Mary*

*F*orget the word *divorce* and never let your children see you argue.

— *Ruth*

*H*ave a meeting on a monthly basis to address the question, "So how are we doing? How can I make our life together better?"

— *Jinanne*

The key to a long and interesting marriage is to respect one another's thoughts and ideas. Your life together will never be boring if each partner has input and remembers that your happiest times together will be those when you are without money and all you have in the world is each other.

– Edward

*A*lways remember to wipe the slate clean when a disagreement is over.

— *Joanna*

*P*raise your spouse to everyone. Approach your disagreements with an attitude of consideration not confrontation.

— *Rebeccah*

*A*ccept your mate. The only thing you will get by trying to change him is disappointment. Have a standing date once a week, especially after you've had children.

– Janet

COMMUNICATE!!! Every day stay close—don't lose your skill to talk frankly to each another.

– Barbara

Marry a person you love to talk to. As you get older, her conversational skills will be as important as any other.

– Samuel

The roses, candles, and love letters will one day be few and far between. When it comes to maintaining a happy marriage, friendship must outlive everything else.

– Clint

You're going to have good times, and you're going to have bad times. It's going to feel so good and sometimes it's going to feel so bad, but you will never have a chance if either of you run away. Hold your love close. Realize you can be angry but still love that person with all of your heart.

— *Tracy*

Other Books by H. Jackson Brown, Jr.

A Father's Book of Wisdom

P.S. I Love You

Life's Little Instruction Book™
   (volumes I, II, and III)

Live and Learn and Pass It On
   (volumes I, II, and III)

Wit and Wisdom from the Peanut Butter Gang

The Little Book of Christmas Joys
   (with Rosemary C. Brown and Kathy Peel)

A Hero in Every Heart
   (with Robyn Spizman)

Life's Little Treasure Books
   On Marriage and Family, On Wisdom, On Joy,
   On Success, On Love, On Parenting, Of Christmas Memories,
   Of Christmas Traditions, On Hope, On Friendship, On Fathers,
   On Mothers, On Things That Really Matter, On Simple Pleasures

Kids' Little Treasure Books
   On Happy Families
   On What We've Learned . . . So Far

Life's Little Instructions from the Bible
   (with Rosemary C. Brown)

Life's Little Instruction Book™ *from Mothers to Daughters*
   (with Kim Shea)